The Loc Princess

Written and Illustrated By Leyetta Cole Batchelor

ISBN:978-0-578-44012-5

For my family

I wrote this story to deal with the insecurities that people may encounter. I found great comfort in positive affirmations and reading the Bible. I hope this book will lift you up in times your feeling down.

"You are fearfully and wonderfully made."

Once upon a time, there was a beautiful Loc Princess that lived in a castle high up on the hillside. The king and queen called her Brianna. Brianna was very beautiful and soft-spoken. Her eyes were brown and easy to gaze upon. Her hair was long and wooly to the touch. Her smile, radiant and bright, it lights up any room she walks into.

There was only one problem, she didn't feel beautiful. Whenever she gets that feeling, she closes her eyes and think about what her mother, the queen, always told her, "You are smart, you are loved, you are beautiful. Never think you're beautiful, know you're beautiful."

As time went on the Loc Princess became very sad. She could not understand why she was feeling the way she was. Everything that she tried to do was stopped because of the overwhelming feeling of sadness.

The next day, it was bright and breezy on the hillside of the castle. The Loc Princess set out early to pick flowers near the stream by the valley. As she walked, she couldn't help but hear a rustle in the grass. "Who's there?" She asked. But there was no answer. So, she continued on her way.

 She finally reached the stream by the valley. She took notice of a young girl on the other side singing a beautiful lullaby. "I am smart, I am loved, I am beautiful." The Loc Princess called out to the young girl, "hello, my name is Brianna, that is a beautiful lullaby you're singing." But when she turned around Brianna was in shock. "Who are you?" Exclaimed Brianna! The young girl answered, hello! My name is Tianna.

Tianna was also very beautiful and soft-spoken. Her eyes were brown and easy to gaze upon just like Brianna's. Her hair was long and wooly to the touch just like Brianna's. Her smile was radiant and bright just like Brianna's. With tears racing down her face, Tianna said "walk with me and I will tell you what I know." So, Tianna set Brianna down and told her all she knew.

One day we were playing with Ms. Lorenz and our mother the queen in the west wing of the castle. The door swung open and the men came in and separated us.

I was allowed to stay with Ms. Lorenz. I was so sad at times, but Ms. Lorenz would sing the song our mom, the queen, use to sing to us as babies, "You are smart, you are loved, you are beautiful." She never let me give up on finding my way back home.

Brianna stated with tears in her eyes, now I remember! It was hard not having you around. I tried not to think about you. "I understand", Tianna said. Can we meet here tomorrow at the same time? Yes! Brianna said excitingly.

Tears flowed down Brianna's face as she thought of how they became separated as small children. The Loc Princess now understood why she was so sad. So she closed her eyes and thought about what her mother the queen always told her, "You are smart, you are loved, you are beautiful, never think you're beautiful, know you're beautiful."

Brianna decided not to speak about what happened while picking flowers near the stream. She went to her room and started to sing. Then it happened, she believed what she was saying. I AM SMART! I AM LOVED! I AM BEAUTIFUL! I AM WHO I SAY I AM!

Finger Play

"I Am"

I am smart – (Flick the index finger up and out)
 I am loved – (Cross your arms on your chest)
I am Beautiful – (thumb pointing at your chin and fingers pointing up. Round your fingers across the front of your face.)
I don't think that I am – (pointing to head)
 I know that I am – (pointing to head)
 I am beautiful - (thumb pointing at your chin and fingers pointing up. Round your fingers across the front of your face.)

57233440R00015

Made in the USA
Columbia, SC
07 May 2019